in the courtyard
of the moon

in the courtyard
of the moon

selected poems
Humberto Ak'bai

translated by
Miguel Rivera
with Fran Quinn

TIA CHUCHA PRESS

Book Design: Jane Brunette
Cover photography design: Michael Rey
Photographs: Juan Rivera, Guatemala
            Gabrielle Rivera-Weissman, Japan
            Mayulí Bieri, Humberto Ak'abal
Illustrations: Gabrielle Rivera-Weissman

Additional translations: Eileen Veronica Rivera, Rick Gutiérrez
Editing: Roshan McArthur

Published by:
Tía Chucha Press
A project of Tía Chucha's Centro Cultural, Inc.
PO Box 328
San Fernando, CA 91341
www.tiachucha.org

Distributed by:
Northwestern University Press
Chicago Distribution Center
11030 South Langley Avenue
Chicago IL 60628

Tía Chucha's Centro Cultural & Bookstore is a 501 (c) (3) nonprofit corporation funded in part over the years by the Arts for Justice Fund, National Endowment for the Arts, California Arts Council, Los Angeles County Arts Commission, Los Angeles Department of Cultural Affairs, The California Community Foundation, the Annenberg Foundation, the Weingart Foundation, the Lia Fund, National Association of Latino Arts and Culture, Ford Foundation, MetLife, Southwest Airlines, the Andy Warhol Foundation for the Visual Arts, the Thrill Hill Foundation, the Middleton Foundation, Center for Cultural Innovation, John Irvine Foundation, Not Just Us Foundation, Liberty Hill Foundation, the Attias Family Foundation, and the Guacamole Fund, among others. Donations have also come from Bruce Springsteen, John Densmore of The Doors, Jackson Browne, Lou Adler, Richard Foos, Gary Stewart, Charles Wright, Adrienne Rich, Tom Hayden, Dave Marsh, Jack Kornfield, Jesus Trevino, David Sandoval, Gary Soto, Sandra Cisneros, Denise Chávez and John Randall of the Border Book Festival, Luis & Trini Rodríguez, and others.

Contents

1

introduction 11

Para quienes / For those 18

Los murciélagos y yo / The bats and I 20

Abril de 1997 / April 1997 22

Viento callado / Silent wind 24

Sin nombre / Without name 26

Los colores / Colors 28

A veces ríos / Sometime rivers 30

Trago de sombra / Sip of shadow 32

En la voz / In the voice 34

Las flores amarillas de los sepulcros / The yellow flowers of the graves 36

El canto viejo de la sangre / The old song of the blood 48

Dolor a flor de rostro / Pain blooms in the face 50

Un libro / A book 52

2

Ri q'ij 57

El sol / The sun 58

De rodillas / On my knees 60

Canto / *Song* 62

Cuando la noche / *When the night* 64

Su tinaja / *Her water jar* 66

Nocheluna / *Moon night* 68

Una puerta / *One door* 70

Creo / *I believe* 72

Hay momentos / *There are moments* 74

Las fotos / *The photos* 76

La tumba / *The tomb* 78

Pueblos extraños / *In orange* 80

La sombra esa / *That one shadow* 82

Color de sol / *Color of the sun* 84

Antes yo ladraba / *I barked* 86

El colibri y la rama / *After the rain* 88

Hay quienes esperan / *Those who wait* 90

Soñé con escribir / *I dreamt about writing* 92

¿Alguna vez? / *Sometime?* 94

Resplandor / *Brightness* 96

Camisa verde / *Green shirt* 98

Los ríos platican / *The rivers talk* 100

Humo blanco / *White smoke* 102

Las miradas azules / *The blue gazes* 104

La neblina / *The fog* 106

Los tecolotes cantan / *The owls sing* 108

La lluvia / *The rain* 110

3

Venezia / *Venice* 114

Ciudad inconclusa / *Unfinished city* 116

Gabbiano e mare 118

Venezia sin adiós / *Venice without goodbye* 120

El fuego de tu aliento / The fire of your breath 122

Luz y sombra / Light and shadow 124

En la estación / At the station 126

Un barco de piedra / A stone ship 128

4

La lengua / The language 132

El baño / The bath 134

La flautista / The flute player 136

La ceremonia / The ceremony 138

Misterio / Mystery 140

En Kyoto / I was told 142

Caricia de luna / Caress of the moon 144

Sólo una vez más / Only one more time 146

La del kimono / She of the kimono 148

En Asákusa / In Asákusa 150

El trueno / Thunder 152

Hieizan 154

La campana de Sandaiakushi / The bell of Sandaiakushi 156

Las maletas / The suitcases 158

No quiero palabras / No words 160

5

El nudo / A knot 164

Sajadura / The slash 166

Mi amor por vos / My love for you 168

Frente a la noche / In front of the night 170

Manos / Hands 172

La poesía / Poetry 174

La luna es la mamá / *The moon is the mother* 176

Los trapos viejos / *Hand me downs* 178

El último hilo / *The last thread* 180

Años / *Years* 182

En Chiantla / *In Chiantla* 184

Todo el día fue de lluvia / *The whole day was rain* 186

Dueños de la noche / *Owners of the night* 188

La caja del muerto / *The box for the dead one* 190

Tuerta / *One eyed* 192

Cuando yo estaba / *When I was* 194

Una enorme corriente / *A huge torrent* 196

Estos poemas / *These poems* 198

La respuesta / *The answer* 200

6

Muqunajik 205

Enterrado / Buried 206

Glossary 209

K'iché pronunciation guide 211

This book is dedicated to the spirit with which the poetry was written.
It is my hope that despite the pitfalls encountered in translation,
its essence will still come across.

A pesar de las deficiencias que pueda haber en la traducción, es mi deseo que
en el libro esté presente el espíritu con que se escribió esta poesía,
al que dedico este trabajo.

Kieb'tzij. Wene man xin kwintaj che uqaxik ruk'juntira ucholaj wa jun
chak wa', ri ku reye'j riwanima, are' che ri uk'ux re wa jun.
Tz'ib'anik wa'kana'tak'ulo ruk' ri
Niuchuq'ab' re xikoj che uchaqu xic.

WITH GRATITUDE TO:

Mayulí Bieri
Nakil Ak'abal
Robert and Ruth Bly
Stephanie Franz-Rivera
Eileen Verónica Rivera
Tomás Rivera
Fran Quinn
Luis Rodriguez
Juan Rivera
Gabrielle Rivera-Weissman
Michael Rey
Rick Gutierrez
Roshan McArthur
Tim Liu
Eleanor Wilner
Minnesota Men's Conference
The Great Mother Conference

Introduction

IN THE SPRING OF 2003, I found myself at a street fair in Los Ángeles, trying to sell copies of Humberto's first collection of poems published in the United States. The event had been called Eco Maya (as in 'reverberation', not short for 'ecology') in the hopes of bringing together in this huge metropolis, the many immigrants and refugees not only from Guatemala but from other Latin American countries as well.

I was placed in a booth between a travel agency and a funeral services company, both selling trips and services to destinations unknown, both run by the Catholic Church. As the day progressed, I was able to reflect on several of the events I was witnessing. In Guatemala 40 years ago, everything that was Maya or Indigenous was despised on many levels, and here at this time in the United States, of all places, it seemed to be the main element that brought all these people together. Many former inhabitants of Guatemala had to travel to this country to see, accept and finally understand the beauty, richness and elegance of a culture that had existed long before the Spanish Conquest, and how it has managed to survive and evolve through the centuries to this day.

A woman picked up one of the books and, after about a half hour of going through the poems, she told me they were too short. "I will not sell you the book," I replied. After more than 20 years of reading the poems, I never tire of them and am always amazed at how much imagery, feeling and beauty are condensed into each one.

The event took place over Easter weekend and, as I was sitting in my booth on Sunday, I realized how the land had mischievously seeded itself in the culture and in all of those attending, and ironically the resurrection taking place inside each one of us had to do with connecting to a place of earth origin on this continent, and not to some religious belief spawned in a desert halfway across the globe two thousand years ago.

In preparing for this edition, I had to consider how much to explain the particulars of Guatemala's life and history to avoid confusion. Ultimately, I believe there is still a misunderstanding of the issues about the conflict in Guatemala here in the United States to this day, so I feel it is appropriate to provide some context here.

FROM 1956 TO 1996, Guatemala was immersed in a long, bloody and bitter civil war, affecting people on all levels of society, its beginning rooted in the 1954 military coup backed by the CIA and the United Fruit Company. During those 40 years of warfare, there was a gradual dehumanization of individuals, due in large part to the relentless and continuous violence. It became acceptable to find dead, mangled bodies in the streets and witness people getting kidnapped, tortured and robbed on a daily basis. A certain numbness began, and it has continued to grow, reflecting the hopelessness felt by a large number of individuals.

The native population has been subjected to exploitation and domination since the arrival of the first Europeans in 1523. Whether it was by plantation owners or the hordes of Christianizing missionaries, this suppressed indigenous life in all of its forms, creating a sterilization of the native culture in some communities. During the years of the Civil War, many political factions were fighting each other, including up to five different rebel groups, the military, and private militias funded by the oligarchy. Innocent civilians were massacred. Political prisoners, artists, writers, doctors, lawyers, engineers, teachers, and students were kidnapped and tortured. All forms of educators and professionals were terrorized, leaving a void in the country at every level.

Even members of religious orders were kidnapped, tortured, and killed. Charity workers and journalists suffered the same fate. In many instances, the military would pose as rebels in order to create confusion. As the conflict continued and economic conditions worsened, people began to rob and kidnap as a way of making a living. They posed either as rebels or soldiers, depending on the circumstances, adding more confusion to the struggle in the political arena. Fleeing the violence, many Guatemalans crossed the border into México, ending up in refugee camps, or living in the wild, hiding by day and foraging at night. Others made the perilous journey to large cities like Los Ángeles in the United States and, in adopting the ways of the country, were introduced to the gang culture.

AFTER THE 1996 PEACE ACCORDS were signed, there was no abatement of the violence people had become accustomed to, due in part to the influx of repatriated gang members from the United States and several drug cartels setting up operations in the country.

When a country suffers from constant waves of violence, it is reflected in the collective at a high level of numbness and disorientation. Many things are left unattended, roads, buildings, bridges, houses, and people. There is no reliable system of laws. The courts are corrupt, making the law of the gun prevail where common sense and respect for human life had been the norm.

There is little or no accountability on the part of individuals in positions of authority, as in the case of Efraín Ríos Montt, one of the many military men responsible for the deaths of thousands (and oddly enough a devout Evangelical Christian). When people do speak up demanding it, they were retaliated against and killed, as in the case of Bishop Juan Gerardi, the founding director of the Guatemalan Archdiocese's Office of Human Rights. Guatemala and many other Latin American countries were pawns in the battle for control of the region between the United States and the Soviet Union.

Until the signing of the Peace Accords in 1996, it was almost an automatic death sentence to talk about what was going on in the country. As a result, anything written reflecting the reality had to be conveyed in a covert manner. The mention of a city or a date, without referring to the particulars of the incident, was sufficient for those reading a poem or article, or listening to a song, to understand the implication. Most of the poems in the first section of the book that refer to the conditions in the country during the war were written after the Peace Accords.

Despite these and many other adversities, it is amazing to find in the land and its people an incredible heart and a hope for life. I believe that this is strongly reflected in Humberto's poems. On reading a draft of this book, poet Eleanor Wilner told me, "I was moved by his voice, its way of embodying the life of a people, history as experienced and emotion shared through his always apt and often astonishing images, and his very concise, compressed language whose constraint tells so much with so few words."

THE POEMS in this collection have been selected from the following volumes:

Retoño salvaje (1997, México)
Desnuda como la primera vez (1998, México)
Con los ojos después del mar (2000, México)

Ovillos de seda (2000, Guatemala)

Gaviota y sueño (2000, Guatemala)

Detrás de las golondrinas (2002, México)

Wachibal q'ijil - Las caras del tiempo (2017, México)

The poems about life in Guatemala are written in K'iché first and then translated into Spanish by Humberto. Poems from all other countries are written in Spanish only. As a reference, there are K'iché versions of some poems included.

Much has changed in this world since the first version of the introduction was written in Boulder, Colorado in 2016; the most significant one being the untimely death of Humberto in January 2019. All I am moved to add at this time is that his poems are needed even more today given the monumental task we have ahead of us in restoring elegance, beauty, eloquence, grace and civility to the world in the years to come.

MIGUEL RIVERA
LOS ÁNGELES, CALIFORNIA
OCTOBER 2020

Para quienes

Para quienes

1

Para quienes

Para quienes
no hablan nuestras lenguas

somos invisibles.

For those

For those
who do not speak our languages

we are invisible.

Los murciélagos y yo

Los murciélagos y yo
esperábamos la llegada
de la noche
para jugar con las estrellas
en el patio de la luna.

The bats and I

The bats and I
waited the arrival
of the night
to play with the stars
in the courtyard of the moon.

Abril de 1997

Y yo creí
que ya no acarreaban
a los campesinos en camiones.

Hoy
los he visto salir de
Santa María Nebaj;
con sus chuchos,
con sus pollos,
con sus remiendos,
con sus tristezas,
con su pedazo de esperanza...

April 1997

And I thought
they did not carry
workers away in trucks anymore.

Today
I saw them leaving
Santa María Nebaj;
with their dogs,
with their chickens,
with their patches,
with their sorrows,
with their piece of hope...

Viento callado

Al día siguiente
de lo que había ocurrido,

el viento pasó callado,
no se atrevía a contar
lo que había visto.

El miedo
caminaba en el aire.

Así amaneció aquel día
cuando la guerra
llegó a estas tierras.

Silent wind

The day after
 it happened,

the wind went by quietly,
it did not dare tell
what it had seen.

Fear
walked in the air.

That is how the day began
when the war
came to these lands.

Sin nombre

No podré olvidar
el ladrido de los chuchos
cuando comían
a los muertos
que se quedaron tirados
en los caminos.

Los chuchos
también se comieron mi nombre.

Without name

I will never forget
the barking of the dogs
as they were eating
the bodies of the dead
left on the roads.

The dogs
also ate my name.

Los colores

Si tuvieran que pintar
la guerra,

¿De qué color la pintarían?

Una dijo de verde;
otra, de rojo;
y otra, de negro.

Colors

If war
were to be painted,

what color would it be?

A woman said green;
another, red;
and another, black.

A veces ríos

Si llevan agua
son ríos

si no,
son caminos.

Sometimes rivers

If they carry water
they are rivers

if not,
they are roads.

Trago de sombra

Sin pensar en el hacha
crecen los árboles;
celan los caminos.

Los caminantes saben
que es beber
un trago de sombra.

Sip of shadow

Without thinking about the ax
the trees grow,
guarding the roads.

The travelers know
what it is to drink
a sip of shadow.

En la voz

En las voces
de los árboles viejos
reconozco las de mis abuelos.

Veladores de siglos.
Su sueño está en las raíces.

In the voice

In the voices
of the old trees
I recognize those of my grandfathers.

Guardians of the centuries.
Their dreams are in the roots.

Las flores amarillas de los sepulcros

Aúllan coyotes y rompen la noche:
pelean con el viento.
«Es mala seña... »
Antes los tecolotes
cantaban de vez en cuando,
ahora cantan cada rato.
«Es mal agüero... »

Un viento de muerte baja de la cumbre,
helado, muerde como chucho con
rabia...
Y las flores se agachan, tienen miedo
y antes del mediodía se marchitan.

Si pudiéramos regresar a aquellos
tiempos
cuando la tierra cantaba con los
hombres.

Hoy los vástagos son cortados de tajo,
los gritos de los chiquitos
a nadie conmueven, a nadie importan:
el cielo abre su boca y traga
el grito que ahoga la muerte.

¿Por qué somos perseguidos los indios?
¿Qué te hemos hecho, Guatemala?
¿Por qué ese odio, esa sed de sangre...?

Nosotros no le debemos nada a la
muerte.

The yellow flowers of the graves

Coyotes howl and shatter the night:
they fight with the wind.
«It is a bad sign... »

In the old days
owls sang once in a while,
now they sing almost all the time
«It is bad luck... »

A death wind descends from the mountaintop,
cold, it bites
like a dog with rabies....
And the flowers bend, scared
and wither before midday.

If we could only go back
to those days
when the Earth
sang with man.

Today saplings are slashed,
the screams of children
don't bother anybody, nobody cares:
the sky opens its mouth and swallows
the shout that death drowns.

Why are we Indians persecuted?
What have we done to you Guatemala?
Why the hatred, the thirst for blood... ?

We do not owe anything
to death.

¿A donde ir, por qué huir?
Si aquí se asentaron nuestros
antepasados,
aquí nacieron nuestros abuelos,
aquí nacieron nuestros padres,
aquí nacímos y aquí nacerán nuestros
hijos;
esta tierra es nuestra.
¿Por qué buscar refugio en otra parte?
¿Por qué hemos de ser peregrinos?

Pajaritos de los barrancos:
Güis güil, Tuc tuc, Chaper pantuj,
vengan a llorar conmigo,
mi tristeza es grande
y la herida duele.

Nuestro cacaxte lleno de sufrimientos,
nos escondemos para que no se burlen
de nuestro llanto,
ahogamos nuestro lloro en los ríos.

¿Acaso es delito ser indio?
Desde 500 años viene esta
persecución.
Matan indios bajo cualquier pretexto:
han borrado pueblos y aldeas enteras.

Señor de los cielos,
Señor de la tierra:
¿En dónde estás cuando pasan estas cosas,
por qué consentís a los asesinos...?

Somos pobres pero trabajadores,
nuestro pecado es ser honrados.

Where do we go, why try to escape?
If here
our ancestors sat,
here our grandfathers were born,
here our fathers were born,
here we were born and here
our children will be born;
this land is ours.
Why look for refuge somewhere else?
Why do we have to be pilgrims?

Birds from the ravines:
Güis güil, Tuc tuc, Chaper pantuj,
come and weep with me,
my sadness is big
and the wound hurts.

Our cacaxte is full of suffering; we hide
so they won't mock us
for weeping;
we drown our cries in the rivers.

Is it a crime to be an Indian?
This persecution began
500 years ago.
Indians are killed under any pretext:
entire towns and villages have been erased.

Lord of the skies,
Lord of the earth:
where are you when these things happen,
why do you favor the murderers . . . ?

We are poor but work hard,
our sin is being honest.

Vivimos en la miseria y en la tristeza
y aún así, resistiendo desde nuestra
cultura.

¿De donde vino esta maldición?
¿De donde salió este remolino
con garras de animal grande,
con ojos que parecen barrancos sin
fondo,
que apaga vidas
para mantener la oscuridad del terror...?

Los animales de los montes se pelean
pero no se matan entre sí.

¡Que estallen los volcanes!
¡Que arrojen fuego!
¡Que tiemble, que se raje la tierra
y se trague todo, todo, todo...!

Aquí nadie quiere paz,
aquí hay hambre de muerte,
los hombres están ciegos,
las leyes están sordas,
los caminos están torcidos...
La noche no da muestras de acabar,
la muerte anda borracha hartándose
de sangre,
las sombras del crimen
extienden sus alas y tapan la luz,
murciélagos danzan entre llamas de
odio:
        ¡Fuego negro!

We live in misery and sadness
and even so
our culture
is our resistance.

Where did this curse
come from?
Where did this
tornado emerge
with the talons of a beast,
with eyes that seem
like black holes,
destroying lives
to maintain the darkness of terror ...?

The animals of the mountains fight
but do not murder each other.

May the volcanoes explode!
May they hurl fire!
May everything tremble, may the earth crack
and swallow it all, all, all... !

Here
nobody wants peace; here
there is hunger for death,
men are blind, laws are deaf; the roads crooked . . .
Night gives no signs of being over,
death walks drunk
engorging itself with blood,
the shadows of crime
spread their wings and cover the light,
bats dance
in the flames of hatred:
Black fire!

¿Jawchí coj be wi? Chi xe coj'iwi ri q'a mam,
chi xe co'jiwí ri q'a tat,
chi xoj alaxicwí...

La justicia no habla en lengua de indios,
la justicia no desciende de los pobres,
la justicia no usa caites,
la justicia no camina descalza
por caminos de tierra...

Gritos aquí,
gritos allá,
gritos por todos lados,
la prepotencia se impone:
pela los dientes;
y nosotros aldeanos y puebleros
tragándonos
la saliva amarga de nuestra impotencia,
sin poder defendernos más que
con nuestros humildes pechos
desnudos.

Caminamos por calles,
caminos y callejones con miedo:
¿quién va adelante, quién viene atrás,
qué fue ese ruido...?
cualquier sombra provoca sobresalto,
el aleteo de un zopilote asusta,
hasta la caída de una hoja
nos hace temblar el alma.

¿Jawchi coj be wi? Chi xe coj'iwi ri q'a mam,
chi xe co'jiwi ri q'a tat,
chi xoj alaxicwi...

Justice does not speak
in the language of Indians,
justice does not
come down to the poor,
justice
does not wear sandals,
justice does not walk
barefoot
on dirt roads.

Screams here,
screams there,
screams everywhere,
arrogance dominates: it skins teeth;
and we the villagers and townspeople
swallow
the bitter spit
of our impotence;
with only our humble naked chests
we are barely able to
defend ourselves.

Who is in front, who is behind,
what was that noise?
We walk through the streets,
roads and alleys in fear:
any shadow will startle,
the wing flaps of a vulture frighten,
even a falling leaf
makes our souls tremble.

Se han abierto los portones del mal
y los mandaderos de la muerte
andan de noche y de día
haciendo matazones...

Las cumbres están llenas de Coxguaj:
«flor amarilla de los sepulcros»
y la tarde amarilla
igual que la flor de muerto
muere detrás de la loma.

¡Sol!
volvete humo, tizná el cielo,
quemá la tierra,
estamos de duelo,
mi gente,
mi sangre,
mi pueblo...

El horizonte gris es triste.
Aquí se ha perdido la vergüenza,
fuego arde en los caminos,
pobreza, hambre y soledad
se arrastran sobe el polvo.
Los patojitos mastican miserias
y tragan sustos, corren sin saber hacia
donde:
¡qué doloroso es ser huérfano!

En ests país de analfabetas
no podemos presumir de ateos:
¿pero,entonces, en qué «Dios»
creen esos que no respetan la vida
humana?

The mountain peaks are covered with Coxguaj:
«yellow flower of the graves»
and the golden afternoon
like the flower of the dead
dies behind the hill.

Sun!
Turn into smoke, smear the sky,
burn the earth,
we are in mourning,
my people,
my blood,
my village...

The gray horizon is sad.
All shame is lost,
fires burn in the roads,
poverty, hunger and loneliness
drag themselves in the dust.
The little children chew miseries
sswalow fear,
run and don't know where:
to be an orphan is to be pain itself!

In this country of illiterates
we cannot pretend to be atheists:
but then, in what «God»
do those who don't respect human life
believe?

Somos muchos,
nuestra presencia no se puede negar,
callados pero no mudos:
las chirimías,
los tambores,
las marimbitas rurales,
las cofradías, los bailes de
enmascarados
en las fiestas de nuestros pueblos...
¿No son acaso la voz
de nuestra existencia?
¿No son la muestra de nuestro amor
por la tranquilidad y la paz...?

En este país nos ven
sólo para fines egoistas:
los politicos se paran sobre nosotros,
los terratenientes nos explotan,
las religiones nos confunden,
y las oficinas de turismo nos exhiben...

Todo esto me desgarra el corazón.
Hermano,
tomémonos este vaso de agua clara,
cantemos aquel cantito del sanate,
démonos un abrazo, olvidá tu tristeza
apenas te puedo mirar entre mis
lágrimas
buscá hoy tu contento
porque mañana...
        ¡quién sabe..!

There are many of us,
our presence cannot be denied,
silent but not mute:
the chirimías,
the drums,
the small rural marimbas,
the cofradías,
the dances of the masks
in the feasts of our villages...
Are they not
the voice of our existence?
Are they not proof of our love
for peace and tranquility?

In this country we are seen
only for selfish ends:
the politicians step on us,
the landowners exploit us,
religions confuse us,
and the tourism agencies exhibit us...

All this tears my heart.
Brother,
let us drink this glass of clear water,
let us sing that little song of the wren,
let us hug, forget your sadness
for I can barely see you through
my tears,
look for your happiness today
because tomorrow...
            who knows!

El canto viejo de la sangre

Yo no mamé la lengua castellana
cuando llegué al mundo.

Mi lengua nació entre árboles
y tiene sabor de tierra;
la lengua de mis abuelos es mi casa.

Y si uso esta lengua que no es mía,
lo hago como quien usa una llave nueva
y abre otra puerta y entra a otro mundo
donde las palabras tienen otra voz
y otro modo de sentir la tierra.

Esta lengua es el recuerdo de un dolor
y la hablo sin temor ni vergüenza
porque fue comprada
con la sangre de mis ancestros.

En esta nueva lengua
te muestro las flores de mi canto,
te traigo el sabor de otras tristezas
y el color de otras alegrías...

Esta lengua es sólo una llave más
para cantar el canto viejo de mi sangre.

The old song of the blood

My mother's breast did not feed me Castillian
when I came into this world.

My language was born among trees
and has the taste of earth;
my ancestor's language is my home.

And if I use this language that is not mine,
I do it as one who uses a new key
and opens a new door and enters another world
where the words have a different voice
and another way of feeling the Earth

This new language is a memory of a pain
and I speak it without fear or shame
because it was earned
with the blood of my ancestors.

In this new language
I show you the flowers of my song
I bring you the taste of other sadnesses
and the color of different joys.

This language is only one more key
to sing the old song of my blood.

Dolor a flor de rostro

Y otra vez la llama del recuerdo
vuelve a encenderme la memoria...

Con el dolor a flor de rostro,
con la mirada hecha pedazos,
mi gente
con sus uñas escarba la tierra

y la madre tierra descubre sus muertos
y los huesos salen a gritar,
a contar con voz de espanto
el terror de esos días,
de esos años, de ese siglo
apenas terminado ayer...

Y el viento desparrama el eco:
Ajkamisanel, ajkamisanel, ajkamisanel... !
Asesinos, asesinos, asesinos... !

Si los huesos de los muertos hablan
por qué vamos a callar los vivos?

Que su memoria se mantenga encendida
y que la llama del recuerdo
no se apague nunca...

No más sangre,
no más dolor,
nunca más...

A LA ORILLA DE UNA FOSA ABIERTA. NEBAJ, 2000.

Pain blooms in the face

Once more a flame returns
and revives my memory...

With pain blooming in the face,
with a shattered gaze,
my people
with their nails dig into the ground

and the earth mother reveals her dead
and bones rise up to cry out,
to tell as only the dead can
the terror of those days,
of those years, of that century
barely over yesterday...

And the wind scatters the echo:
Ajkamisanel, ajkamisanel, ajkamisanel... !
Murderers, murderers, murderers... !

If the bones of the dead speak
how can we the living stay silent?

May their memory stay alive
and may the flame of remembrance
never go out...

No more blood,
no more pain,
never more...

AT THE SIDE OF AN OPEN GRAVE. NEBAJ, 2000
Translated by: Miguel Rivera, Eileeen Veronica Rivera, Rick Gutiérrez

Un libro

Como deseo que llegue el día
cuando en este país
todos anduvieran armados
de un libro.

A book

How I wish for the day to come
when in this country
all walk around armed
with a book.

2

Ri q'ij

Ri q'ij
kunim rib'
chu uxo'l ri xot

ruk' ri ujanalik
xa karaj kuril
jas k'o chupan
re ri qachoch

ka saqmaqi'k
are jampa' kurilo
ruk ri uchaj, ri usaqil
che sib'alaj saq
ri qameb'ayil.

El sol

El sol
se mete
entre tejas

con esa terquedad
de mirar
que hay
dentro de nuestras casitas.

Y se pone pálido
al ver
que con su luz
es más clara
nuestra pobreza.

The sun

The sun
gets in between
the roof tiles

with that stubbornness
of wanting to see
what is
inside our little houses.

And he goes pale
on seeing
that our poverty
is more obvious
in his light.

De rodillas

¿Por que viniste
a interrunpir mi vida?

¿Quién te envió,
cómo has podido meterte
en mi corazón?

Ya no puedo arrancarte
de mí.

Ya no puedo vivir
sin tu aliento.

Ni siquiera puedo
ponerme de pie.

Poesía, ya ves,
estoy de rodillas.

On my knees

Why did you come
to interrupt my life?

Who sent you?
How were you able to get
inside my heart?

I cannot
tear you out of me.

I cannot live
without your breath.

I cannot even
stand up.

Poetry, I am
on my knees.

Canto

El abuelo, de la mano,
lleva a su nieto
a saludar a los árboles,
a platicar con ellos,
a acariciar su piel,
a oler sus hojas...

Y los árboles
cantan sus nombres.

Song

The grandfather,
takes his grandson by the hand
to greet the trees,
talk to them, feel their skin
smell their leaves...

And the trees
sing their names.

Cuando la noche

Cuando la noche es fría
los tecolotes
encienden luciérnagas
para calentar sus patas.

When the night

When the night is cold
the owls
light up fireflies
to warm their feet.

Su tinaja

Su carita
color de madrugada.

De la casa a la poza
de la poza a la casa.

Ella
tapa su tinaja
con la luna llena.

Her water jar

Her small face
the color of dawn.

From the house to the well,
from the well to the house.

She
covers the mouth of her water jar
with the full moon.

Nocheluna

Por la ventana
habían entrado las estrellas,
cuidaban tu sueño.

La luna te lamía la cara.

Y en tu boca, Mayulí,
Una abeja no dormía:

fabricaba un beso.

Moon night

Through the window
stars came in,
guarding your sleep.

The moon licked your face.

And on your mouth, Mayulí,
a bee far from sleeping

was making a kiss.

Una puerta

Mi corazón
sólo tiene una puerta

y se abre por fuera.

One door

My heart
has only one door

and it opens
from the outside.

Creo

Creo más en alguien
capaz de recordar

que en alguien que me diga
que puede olvidar.

I believe

I believe more in somebody
able to remember

than somebody who tells me
he can forget.

Hay momentos

Hay momentos en la vida
en que las lágrimas
son incapaces de liberar
el dolor en el corazón
de el que se va

o del que se queda.

There are moments

There are moments in life
when tears
are not capable of freeing
the pain in the heart
of the one who leaves

or the one who stays.

Las fotos

En esta foto
pareciera que no te cansaras,
estás de pie.

En esta otra,
como si no envejecieras.

Y en estas otras... bueno,
en todas hay algo que no cambia:

tus ojos
siempre están tristes.

The photos

In this photo,
you look like you never get tired,
you're standing up.

In this one, as if
you never get old.

And in these others... well,
in all of them something
does not change:

your eyes
are always sad.

La tumba

Mi papá
me llevaba al cementerio
y allí junto a una tumba
dejaba caer sus ojos.

—No conocí a mi mamá
—me decía—, ella murió
el día que yo nací.

Él arrancaba puños de tierra
y los ponía junto a su corazón.

The tomb

My father
took me to the cemetery

and his eyes fell
next to a grave.

—I never knew my mother—
he said— she died
on the day I was born.

He tore handfuls of dirt from the ground
and put them next to his heart.

Pueblos extraños

El sol baña de naranja
las calles arrugadas
de esos pueblos extraños
que las nubes construyen
en el aire.

In orange

the sun bathes
the wrinkled streets
of those strange cities
clouds make
in the sky.

La sombra esa

La sombra
de esa hoja de nogal
camina sobre la pared
como un murciélago
buscando la oscuridad
debajo del techo de la casa.

Sobre la loma
el sol
envejece un poco

That one shadow

The shadow
of that walnut leaf
walks on the wall
like a bat
looking for darkness
under the roof of the house.

Over the hill,
the sun
ages little by little.

Color de sol

El jaguar es un animal
de color de sol
con parches negros.

Su cola se alarga
hasta la orilla del sueño.

Este animal
a veces llora.

Color of the sun

The jaguar is an animal
the color of the sun
with black patches.

His tail
streaches out
to the edge of the dream.

Sometimes
this animal
weeps.

Antes yo ladraba

Antes yo ladraba
y no recuerdo en qué sueño
se me olvidó esa costumbre.

Ahora
        hablo

I barked

I used to bark
and I can't remember which dream
caused me to forget.

Now
      I speak.

El colibrí y la rama

El colibrí y la rama,
enredados
en los cabellos del sol
después del aguacero.

After the rain

A hummingbird and a branch
tangled
in the hairs of the sun.

Hay quienes esperan

Hay quienes esperan
el fin del mundo;

pobres,
no se han dado cuenta:

hace tiempo
que está hecho pedazos.

Those who wait

There are those who wait for
the end of the world;

poor fools,
they haven't noticed:

for some time
it's been in pieces.

Soñé con escribir

Soñé con escribir
un poema que no dijera nada.

Simplemente
que me recordara algo,

alguien...

desnuda...
como la primera vez.

I dreamt about writing

I dreamt about writing
a poem that said nothing.

Simply
to remind me of something,

somebody...

naked...
like the first time.

¿Alguna vez?

¿Me has pensado alguna vez
en tu corazón?

O ya me perdiste en tu cabeza

Some time?

Am I ever in
your heart?

Or have you
lost me in your head?

Resplandor

Yo te perseguía
en el mercado
como río detrás
de la espuma.

—No soy la única mujer
para que me andés coleando
—me dijiste.

—Sólo hay una luna en el cielo
—te respondí.

—También hay estrellas
—me contestaste.

—Sí, pero las que están
cerca de ella no se ven
porque su resplandor
las desvanece.

Brightness

I followed you
in the market
like a river
chasing foam.

—I am not the only woman.
Stop tailing me,
—you told me.

—There is only one moon in the sky
—I answered.

—There are stars also
—you replied.

—Yes, but the close ones
can't be seen
because her splendor
makes them vanish.

Camisa verde

Me puse
aquella camisa verde,
era un poco vieja.

Y el pantalón,

bueno, el pantalon
tenía algunos remiendos,
pero estaba limpio.

Me paré
debajo de aquel ciprés
donde tienen su nido
los tecolotes grises.

Apareciste
en la curva del camino
y pasaste delante de mí
como si yo hubiera sido
un tecolote más.

Green shirt

I put on
that green shirt.
It was a little worn.

And the pants,

well, the pants
had some patches,
but they were clean.

I stood
under that cypress
where the grey owls
have their nest.

You appeared
on the curve of the road
and passed in front of me

as if I were
one more owl.

Los ríos platican

Los ríos platican con las piedras
cuando los árboles duermen.

Al amanecer
las piedras callan
y los árboles cantan.

The rivers talk

The rivers talk with stones
when trees are sleeping.

At dawn
the stones go silent
and the trees sing.

Humo blanco

En la cocina
los cabellos del abuelo
se mezclan
con el humo blanco
de esa encina verde
que no quiere arder.

Afuera,
la vieja lluvia
va y viene
arrastrada por el viento.

White smoke

In the kitchen,
the hair of the grandfather
blends
with the white smoke
from that green oak
that will not burn.

Outside,
the old rain
comes and goes
dragged around by the wind.

Las miradas azules

Las miradas azules
que nacen en tus ojos
hacen más bellas las horas
de estos días estrechos

y olvido
que me falta el sol.

The blue gazes

The bue gazes
born in your eyes
make beautiful the hours
of these long days

and I forget
I am missing the sun.

La neblina

La neblina,
aliento de los árboles,

se desmadeja
entre las ramas del amanecer.

The fog

The fog,
breath of trees,

unravels
in the branches of dawn.

Los tecolotes cantan

Los tecolotes cantan,
la luna llueve luz,
el cielo se humedece,
nacen estrellas

y los tecolotes
no paran de cantar.

The owls sing

The owls sing,
the moon rains light,
the sky moistens,
stars are born

and the owls
just can't stop singing.

La lluvia

Cuando de noche llueve
las flores salen de paseo,
los árboles
hablan de sus cosas;
cosas de antes

y lloran.

The rain

When it rains at night,
the flowers go out for a stroll—
the trees
talk about their concerns,
things from long ago—

and they weep.

Ciudad inconclusa

3

Venezia

Los mares la quieren
como una barca
que se quedó dormida.

Y la neblina,
aliento del amor,
la mantiene suspendida
entre las alas del viento.

Venice

The oceans love her
like a ship
that stayed asleep.

And the fog,
breath of love,
keeps her suspended
between the wings of the wind.

Ciudad inconclusa

Venezia es una canción en la neblina. Un suspiro
diluido en el agua y en el viento. Una ciudad
inconclusa, siempre se está haciendo. Ella se deja
moldear para que cada quien se haga su propia Venezia
y se la lleve en el corazón. Se deja amar para vivir un
sueño sin ayer ni mañana. Uno se pierde en sus calles,
el corazón se va por un lado y los ojos por el otro; y al
reencontrarse con uno mismo parecieran dos extraños
con dos ciudades distintas bajo el brazo.

¡Cuantas veces me he sentido como una araña
enredada en la tela de esa ciudad maga!

Un mapa no sirve para nada en Venezia.

Unfinished city

Venice is a song in the fog. A breath spread out on the water and the wind. An unfinished city, always making itself. She lets herself be molded so that every one can make his or her own Venice and carry it in the heart. She lets herself be loved in order to live in dreams without a yesterday or a tomorrow. One gets lost in her streets. The heart goes one way and the eyes go the other; and when they meet up with themselves they seem like two strangers with two different cities carried under their arms.

How many times I have felt like a spider tangled in the web of this sorceress city!

A map is worthless in Venice.

Gabbiano e mare

La barca se alejó
y la tarde no quiso verla.

Las gaviotas jugaban
con las brisas del agua.

Y las olas del mar
cantaban;

me voy
me quedo,
me voy
me quedo,
me voy
me quedo...

Quien inventó la despedida
no tenía corazón.

Gabbiano e mare

The boat went away
and the afternoon didn't want to see her.

The gulls played
with the winds of the waters.

And the ocean waves
sang;

I'm going
I'm staying,
I'm going
I'm staying.
I'm going
I'm staying...

Whoever invented goodbyes
didn't have a heart.

Venezia sin adiós

Su cuello de mármol
descansó sobre mis hombros.

Como una gladiola blanca
se deshojó en la estación.

Con la maleta
llena de recuerdos
y conteniendo un grito,
el tren me arrancó
de los brazos de Venezia.

Cada vez más lejos
y sin saber a donde...

Mi corazón se había quedado.

Venezia, Venezia:
yo no puedo decirte adios.

Venice without goodbye

Its neck of marble
rested on my shoulders.

Like a white gladiola
it dropped its petals at the station.

With a suitcase
full of memories
and holding in a scream,
the train ripped me
from Venice's arms.

Each moment farther away
and without knowing where to . . .

My heart stayed behind.

Venice, Venice:

I cannot say goodbye to you.

El fuego de tu aliento

Tus ojos iluminaban las calles por donde paseábamos. Te reías. Cantaba tu voz. Eras un pajarillo silbando de rama en rama. Tomé tu rostro entre mis manos, me sumergí en las aguas marinas de tu profunda mirada: mar inmenso, eco de olas, un barco...

Sentí el calor de tus manos y el fuego de tu aliento. Tú y yo, solos. Así es la dicha, no se necesita sino de dos. Venezia de palacios, puentes, canales, calles, plazas.

Tus labios invitaban a beber tu sonrisa. Me acerqué para robarte un beso. Justo en ese momento sentí que alguien me tocó la espalda. Dí un giro para ver quién era. No había nadie.

Volví a ti, busqué tus labios. No estabas.

Miré hacia todos lados, como un perro di dos o tres vueltas alrededor de mí y nada.

Me quedé mirando la calle aquella que desemboca en tu recuerdo.

The fire of your breath

Your eyes lit the streets where we walked. You laughed. Your
voice sang. You were a bird singing from branch to branch. I
took your face in my hands, I went into the sea waters of
your deep gaze: vast ocean, echoes of waves, a ship . . .

I felt the warmth of your hands and the fire of your breath.
You and I, alone. Such is joy; it only needs two. Venice of
palaces, bridges, canals, streets, plazas.

Your lips invited me to drink at your smile. I came close to
steal a kiss. In that moment I felt someone touch
my back. I turned to see who it was. No one there.

I turned back to you, looked for your lips. You were gone.

I looked everywhere, like a dog I turned myself around two or
three times and nothing.

I kept staring at that street that empties out into the
memory of you.

Luz y sombra

Yo no puedo separarme del recuerdo, andamos como la luz y la sombra. Si lo echara al mar, jamás se ahogaría porque su corazón es de agua y sus olas serían cada vez más altas. Si lo sepultara en tierra, volvería a brotar: es semilla es simiente. Si lo arrojara al viento, su vuelo sería eterno, es ave, sus alas abarcan desde el nacimiento hasta la caída del sol. Y, si lo hechara al fuego, sus llamas nada podrían con él, porque también es fuego y quema.

El recuerdo va delante y yo voy detrás.

Si el recuerdo muere, el futuro también moriría.

Light and shadow

I cannot separate myself from the memory; we walk like the light and the shadow. If I threw him into the ocean, he would never drown because his heart is of water and his waves would be bigger each time. If I buried him in the ground he would sprout again: he is seed, he is semen. If I threw him to the wind, his flight would be eternal; he is a bird, his wings spanning from dawn to dusk. And if I threw him into the fire, his flames could not touch him, for he is also fire and burns.

The memory goes in front and I am behind.

If the memory dies, the future will also die.

En la estación

En la estación
la campana del reloj
rompió nuestro abrazo.

Arrivederci.

Tus ojos desaparecieron,
con la llema de mis dedos
tome una lágrima.

Guardé en mi corazón
una mirada.

El tren me alejó.

At the station

At the station
with the clocks
chiming
I let you go.

Arrivederci.

Your eyes were gone.
With my fingertips
I took a tear.

I hid a glance
in my heart.

And the train
took me away.

Un barco de piedra

Venezia es un barco de piedra
anclada en el mar.

Venice

A stone ship
anchored in the sea.

4

La lengua

La lengua Japonesa
es un ovillo de seda
entre las patas de un gato.

The language

The Japanese language
is a little ball of silk
between the paws of a cat.

El baño

La desnudez
desaparece con la luz
transparente del agua.

El baño Japonés
al final de la tarde
suaviza hasta el alma.

Y el sueño desciende
como el rocío sobre la
hierba.

The bath

I am clothed
only
in the water's light.

At the end of the day,
this Japanese bath
softens everything
right down to the soul.

And sleep descends
like dew over
the grass.

La flautista

Con su cuerpo
de clave de sol,
la flautista ofrece un beso.

Pinta con su pincel de viento
la caída de una gota de té
en el dorado corazón
de un crisantemo.

The flute player

With her body
in the key of the sun,
the flute player offers a kiss.

With her wind-brush she paints
a drop of tea falling onto

the golden heart
of a chrysanthemum.

La ceremonia

Los zapatos
no deben entrar.

El lenguaje de los pies:
la intimidad,
la communión.
el silencio.

Los pies ven hacia en interior.
los zapatos apuntan a la calle;
su idioma son los caminos.

Calzarse
descalzarse,
calzarse,
descalzarse . . .

La ceremonia del zapato
en la puertas del Japón.

The ceremony

The shoes
should not go in.

The language of the feet:
the intimacy, the communion,

the silence.

The feet look inside. The shoes
point toward the street, their language
is the road.

Shoes on, shoes off,
shoes on,
shoes off . . .

A ceremony of shoes
in the doorways of Japan.

Misterio

Hay algo en tu voz
que convierte my lengua en miel.

Mystery

There is something in your voice
that turns my words into honey.

En Kyoto

Me contaron en Kyoto
que las las mangas estrechas
del kimono
dicen con callada voz
que ellas son vírgenes

I was told

in Kyoto
narrow kimono
sleeves say
"virgin"

(in a quiet voice.)

Caricia de luna

La luna acaricia
con su viejo silencio
los cabellos de aquella flor
recostada en la puerta
de su ventana.

Caress of the moon

With its old silence
the moon
fingers the hair
of that flower
leaning on her
window sill.

Sólo una vez más

Enséñame a cantar, alondra,
antes que el sol se vaya.

Déjame escuchar tu voz
antes que la noche llegue.

Sólo ona vez más tus ojos...

Mañana,
cuando el sol vuelva
ya no estará mi sombra.

Only one more time

Teach me to sing, lark,
before the sun goes away.

Let me hear your voice
before the night comes.

Only one more time your eyes . . .

Tomorrow
when the sun returns, my shadow
will be gone.

La del kimono

Sus ojos
de sol semi-oculto,
apenas
dos lineas
bajo el horizonte de sus cejas:
lloraban

Su rostro de piel de luna
iluminada por la luz
de sus cabellos negros:
callaba.

Ella, la del kimono amarillo,
la de las mangas anchas.

She of the kimono

Her eyes
an almost hidden sun,
barely
two lines
below the horizon of her brows:
wept.

Her face the color of the moon
lit from the glow
of her black hair:
silent.

She, in the yellow kimono,
the one with the wide sleeves.

En Asákusa

Fina llovizna de arroz:
lluvia menuda, acariciante;

En Asákusa
invita a mojarse.

El otoño es un mago
encanta irremediablemente.

In Asákusa

Rice like drizzle:
a small, caressing rain

invites one to get wet
in Asákusa.

Fall is
a magician
incurably enchanting.

El trueno

El cielo de Tokyo fue roto
por el estallido de un trueno...

El eco se hizo pedazos.

Las calles de luces
se llenaron de lluvia..

O tal vez la lluvia
se bañó de luces.

Thunder

The sky over Tokyo
blasted by thunder . . .

The echo in pieces.

The light streets
filled with rain.

Or maybe the rain
bathed in lights.

Hieizan

Apenas pasada
un ala de sombra
de la media noche,

tembló en Hieizan,
la montaña sagrada de Buda.

Cantó un pájaro en mi ventana:
piiiyoy, piiiyoy, piiiyoy . . .

Mi corazón dejó de temer
y volví a soñar.

Hieizan

A wing of shadow
barely past
midnight,

trembled in Hieizan
the sacred mountain of Buddah

A bird sang at my window:
piiiyoy, piiiyoy, piiiyoy . . .

My heart stopped quaking
and I returned to the dream.

La campana de Sandaiakushi

POOOOOOMMMMMMMMMMMM . . .
La vieja campana
con su enorme boca
llamando al mundo.

OOOOOOMMMMMMMMMMMM . . .
El eco viaja sobre las montañas
arrastrando la campana.

Mmmmmmmmmmmmmmmmmm . . .
Y se vuelve viento.

The bell of Sandaiakushi

POOOOOOMMMMMMMMMMM . . .
The old bell
with its enormous mouth
calling the world.

OOOOOOMMMMMMMMMMMM . . .
The echo travels over the mountains
dragging the bell.

Mmmmmmmmmmmmmmmmmmm . . .
And slowly turns to wind.

Las maletas

—¿Te vas?
—Aún no.
—¿Y, por qué están echas las maletas?
—Porque soy un viajero
y en cualquier momento
tendré que irme,
no solo de ésta ciudad
sino también de éste mundo.
—¿Y, de mi corazón?
—Sólo si tú abres la puerta.

The suitcases

—Are you leaving?
—Not yet.
—Why then are your bags packed?
—Because I am a traveler
and at any moment
I will have to leave,
not only from this city
but also from this world.
—And, from my heart?
—Only if you open the door

No quiero palabras

Un beso
sólo un beso,
no quiero palabras.

Las palabras
son para cosas innecesarias.

No words

A kiss
only a kiss —
I don't want words.

Words
are useless things.

5

El nudo

Un nudo
que no puedo deshacer

me amarra el corazón

A knot

A knot
I cannot undo

ties up my heart

Sajadura

Ella lo buscó:

no para rogarle
que él cumpliera su promesa
sino para darle otro recuerdo.

Era domingo

y sin decirle una palabra
le sajó la cara
con un cuchillo.

The slash

She looked for him:

not to beg him
to keep his promise

but to give him another memory.

It was Sunday.

Without saying a word,
she slashed his face
with a knife.

Mi amor por vos

Mi amor por vos,
como decirte,

es algo así
como la lengua de un jaguar
lamiendo su cachorro

My love for you

My love for you,
how can I tell you,

is something like
the tongue of a jaguar
licking its cub.

Frente a la noche

Aquí frente a la noche,
frente a la lluvia,
mi corazón entristece.

Soy un pájaro sin una rama,

un pájaro
que busca nido.

In front of the night

Here in front of the night,
in front of the rain,
my heart saddens.

I am a bird without a branch,

a bird
looking for a nest.

Manos

Las veo y me pareece
como si hubieran nacido
antes que ella.

Arrugadas, rústicas,
lejos ya de los trabajos
de aquellos días...

Cómo han envejecido
las manos de mi mamá.

Hands

I look at them
and it seems
they were born
before she ever was.

Wrinkled, coarse,
far away now
from the work of those days...

How my mother's hands
have aged.

La poesía

La poesía, finalmente
me convirtió en un huevón.

Y ahora
no hago
otra cosa
sino escribir.

El caso es que,
aunque quisiera,
a mí ya no me dan trabajo
ni siquiera de sanatero.

Poetry

Poetry, finally,
has turned me into a lazy ass.

And now
I can't do
anything else
but write.

The thing is,
even if I wanted,
nobody
will give me work

not even
as a scarecrow.

La luna es la mamá

La luna es la mamá
de los colores
que no conocen el día,

ella los pinta
al revés.

The moon is the mother

The moon is the mother
of the colors
that don't know the day.

She paints them on everything
backwards.

Los trapos viejos

Los trapos viejos
que los árboles
ya no usarán más

son las hojas
con que se viste el suelo.

Hand-me-downs

The old rags
the trees
will not use anymore

are the leaves
that will dress the ground.

El último hilo

El último hilo
de la luz del día
se arquea
bajo el peso
de la noche
y no se rompe,

se parece a la esperanza.

The last thread

The last thread
of daylight
bends

under the weight
of the night
and does not break,

it resembles hope.

Años

El abuelo
camina con mis pies,
ve con mis ojos,
se recuesta sobre mis hombros;

cómo pesan sus años.

Years

Grandfather
walks with my feet,
sees with my eyes,
leans on my shoulders;

how heavy his years weigh.

En Chiantla

No es el cuerpo,
es el alma de ellas
la que danza.

La marimba
con sus cantos de madera
acaricia esos pies descalzos.

Ellas danzan
en el mismo lugar,

como la llama
sobre su candela
hasta derretirse.

In Chiantla

It is not the body, but
the soul of those women
that is dancing.

The marimbas with their
song of wood
caress those bare feet.

They dance in
the same place,

like the flame on her
candle until

it melts.

Todo el día fue de lluvia

Todo el día fue de lluvia,
al final de la tarde
la noche venía bajando
y no pudo seguir su camino
porque se quedó trabada
en el lodazal.

En el pueblo no hubo noche,
sólo oscuridad.

The whole day was rain

The whole day was rain,
at the end of the afternoon
night was coming down
and could not go on
because she got stuck
in the mud.

In the village there was no night,
only darkness.

Dueños de la noche

Los sueños
cuidan los caminos
de la noche.

Ellos se adelantan
para ver que hay
detrás de las curvas.

Luego regresan
para contarlo
y uno cree que está soñando.

Owners of the night

Dreams
guard the roads
at night.

They go on ahead
to see what is
behind the next turn.

Shortly they return
to give their report.

And that is what
we believe are "dreams."

La caja del muerto

La caja del muerto era
de color de árbol.

Lo dejaron en el cementerio
al lado del silencio
de los demás.

Cuando volvieron a casa,
ella sintió como si se hubiera
liberada del peso
de una piedra.

—Se fue... Se fue...
—les dijo a sus hijos.

Aquel marido la golpeaba.

Ella es mi mama
y él fue mi padre.

The box for the dead one

The box for the dead one
was the color of a tree.

They left him in the graveyard
beside the silence of the others.

When they returned to their home,
she felt as if she had
been freed
from the weight of a stone.

—He went away... he went away...
she told her children.

That husband hit her.

She is my mother
and he was my father.

Tuerta

La luna es tuerta
por eso
no da mucha luz.

One eyed

The moon has only one eye—
that is why
she does not give much light.

Cuando yo estaba

"Cuando yo estaba embarazada,
esperándote,
sentía muchas ganas
de comer tierra;
arrancaba pedacitos
de adobes
y me los comía".

Esta confesión de mi madre
me desgarró el corazón.

Mamé leche de barro,
por eso mi piel
es color de tierra.

When I was

"When I was pregnant,
waiting for you,
I had strong urges
to eat dirt;
I tore off adobe
chunks
and ate them."

This confession from my mother
tore my heart.

I drank clay milk from her breast—
that is why my skin
is the color of the earth.

Una enorme corriente

Una enorme corriente
de agua sucia
pasó aullando por el pueblo.

El río se escondió
y la noche tragó a la lluvia.

Al amanecer,
una tortuga vieja
pataleando en el lodazal
ni sabía en qué pueblo
se encontraba.

A huge torrent

A huge torrent
of dirty water
came howling through the town.

The river hid
and night swallowed the rain.

At dawn,
an old turtle
kicking in the mud
didn't know what village
she was in.

Estos poemas

Estos poemas
han sido escritos
como las veredas de mi pueblo,
a puro pico de piocha
y un poco cada día.

A lo mejor por eso
la naturaleza me dejó cojo
para que yo vaya despacio
detrás de los que van corriendo.

These poems

These poems
have been written
like the paths of my village
with only the point of a pick axe—
a little every day.

Maybe it is better—
nature left me with a limp
so I can go slowly
behind those who run.

La respuesta

—Abrir la tiera
con las manos,
llenarse de su aroma,
levantar el rostro al cielo
y comer el aire:

esa es la paz
—respondió la abuela.

The answer

—Open up the earth
with your hands,
be filled with its scent,
raise your face to the sky
and eat the wind:

that is peace
—the grandmother said.

Enterrado

Enterrado

6

Muqunajik

Xinwoq'ej ri nutat
are jampa xinwaraj ri ukaminaqil,
xinoq'ik are jampa xuyakan ri rachoch
are k'ut xqak'am ri be cho ri jom
chila xinch'abej kanoq.

Xinban ri bis,
are xink'astajik pa numebayil,
xuwi nukutel chik xinwe'tamaj
che we jun ukutel kakanajik,
rajawaxik kumuq kanoq
konojel ri k'exk'ol ri man kato'b taj
che rilik ri uk'aslemal jun.

Enterrado

Lloré a mi padre
mientras velaba su cadaver,
lo lloré cuando el féretro salió de casa
camino al cementerio
y allí le dije adiós.

Hice el duelo,
y al amanecer en mi orfandad,
me ví solo y comprendí
que para vivir solo
necesitaba dejar enterrado con él
todo el dolor que me impidiera
seguir viviendo.

Buried

I wept for my father
during his wake,
I wept when the coffin went out of the house
on the way to the cementery
and there I said goodbye.

I mourned,
and when I awoke as an orphan,
I saw myself alone and understood
that to live I only
needed to leave buried with him
all the pain that could stop me
from living.

GLOSSARY

adobe: sundried brick made of mud and straw

cacaxte: portable wooden structure where objects for sale are displayed. Seen in markets and streets. Also carried by merchants on their backs.

chaper pantuj: woodpecker, colloquial to Momostenango

chirimía: oboe like double reed wind instrument, brought by the Spanish and assimilated into native music

chucho: street mutt

cofradía: Syncretic religious social order combining Maya and Catholic traditions, equivalent to a Medicine Society; members are responsible for maintaining the rituals to the land, its deities and the community.

coxguaj: Tagetes erecta, Aztec marigold

güis güil: golondrina, swallow

Nebaj: Village in the department of Quiché, Guatemala where in 1982 one of the many massacres during the civil war took place, affecting the Maya-Ixil people.

tuc tuc: woodpecker

SIMPLE K'ICHE PRONUNCIATION GUIDE

All of the vowels have the same pronunciation as in Spanish. The same applies to consonants, with some exceptions.

The letters that have a very strong pronunciation without a major variation are q and k. The sound can be emphasized by placing an apostrophe after the letter; x is pronounced sh.

Stress, unless noted, is usually on the final syllable of the word.